Animal Psalms

ANIMAL PSALMS

POEMS BY
Alfred Nicol

ABLE MUSE PRESS

Copyright ©2016 by Alfred Nicol
First published in 2016 by

Able Muse Press

www.ablemusepress.com

All rights reserved. No part of this book may be used or reproduced in any manner whatsoever without written permission except in the case of brief quotations embedded in critical articles and reviews. Requests for permission should be addressed to the Able Muse Press editor at editor@ablemuse.com

Printed in the United States of America

Library of Congress Control Number: 2015955769

ISBN 978-1-927409-69-5 (paperback)
ISBN 978-1-927409-70-1 (digital)

Cover image: "Double Discovery" by Alexander Pepple
(with "harp 06" by Esther Cassinelli, "cat chair" by Brigitte Werner)

Cover & book design by Alexander Pepple

Able Muse Press is an imprint of *Able Muse: A Review of Poetry, Prose & Art*—at www.ablemuse.com

Able Muse Press
467 Saratoga Avenue #602
San Jose, CA 95129

for Gina

Acknowledgments

I am grateful to the editors of the following journals where many of the poems in this collection originally appeared, sometimes in earlier versions:

Alabama Literary Review: "Believe You Me," "Cellar Snake," and "The Passional"

American Arts Quarterly: "Mason Gardner Sold His Place" and "October, 1962"

Angle: "Eel," "Sacred Spring," and "Triptych"

Atlanta Review: "Black Spinet"

Clarion: "Mid-November House Guest"

First Things: "Animal Psalms" and "The Guitar Maker"

The Flea: "Against Beauty"

The Hopkins Review: "A Game in Late August" and "Planning a Rescue"

Ibbetson Street: "The Convert" and "Why Bees Hum"

Light: "Bad Head Day," "Division of Labor," and "Persnickety Ichabod, Class of '74"

Measure: "Applicant Evaluation: Thomas, Dylan," "Doctor B___," and "Reading French"

Merton Seasonal: "Seeds"

Oberon: "Crouch"

Off the Coast: "Free Stuff" and "Genius Is Only Good for What It's Good For"

Per Contra: "The Adversary's Adages," "An Innocence," "Levieux Gets the Best of His Better Sense," "The Regular," and "Worried She May Be the One"

San Diego Reader: "A Bother," "Ellipse," and "One Day"

Think: "Pensées Pourries"

Contents

Acknowledgments	*vi*
A Game in Late August	*3*
Penseés Pourries	*5*
Seeds	*8*
Animal Psalms	*9*
Reading French	*10*
The Regular	*12*
Division of Labor	*13*
Against Beauty	*14*
Crouch	*15*
Levieux Gets the Best of His Better Sense	*16*
The Adversary's Adages	*17*
Mason Gardner Sold His Place	*18*
Worried She May Be the One	*23*
Planning a Rescue	*24*
Free Stuff	*27*
Believe You Me	*28*
Bad Head Day	*30*
Genius Is Only Good for What It's Good For	*31*
Applicant Evaluation: Thomas, Dylan	*32*
Persnickety Ichabod, Class of '74	*33*

An Innocence	*35*
Doctor B___	*36*
Ellipse	*39*
Cellar Snake	*40*
The Passional	*42*
Mid-November House Guest	*44*
January	*46*
October 1962	*47*
Black Spinet	*48*
Eel	*51*
The Convert	*54*
Triptych	*56*
How to Ignore an Invisible Man	*60*
The Guitar Maker	*62*
One Day	*64*
Sacred Spring	*65*
Genius	*67*
A Bother	*70*
Why Bees Hum	*71*
Nuts	*72*

Animal Psalms

A Game in Late August

Seeded last, our boys expect defeat.
Ninety-five degrees. No shade at all.
It's a bad mix: long odds, the brutal heat . . .
The umpire's here and ready, though. Play ball.

Number 8 bends down to tie his cleats.
He's not afraid of a line drive his way,
as are his parents, quiet in their seats.
His brother joined the Army yesterday.

One little cloud in all the glaring sky,
not even drifting, sticks and hangs up there
like gauze over a cut. And a pop fly
just past the fielder's outstretched glove lands fair.

Another error. The cicadas' sound
grows louder as our pitcher comes unglued.
The catcher walks out slowly to the mound.
I guess he speaks of hope and fortitude.

The inning just won't end. They bat around.
Time backs up and idles overhead.
The boy in left is kneeling on the ground.
A change is made. The pitcher's arm is dead.

The new guy walks the next two, then a third,
and there's a portent in the air, a vibe
that says the unavoidable's occurred:
some kid just wished the wish, betrayed the tribe—

he didn't keep the faith, he snuffed the fire,
he left the narrow path and caused the fall—
admitting to the one taboo desire
that summer not be endless after all.

The words, once spoken, cannot be recanted;
the field turns reddish-brown. There and then
the sorcery's complete, the wish is granted.
The game looks more like work; the boys, like men.

And still there are the innings left to play.
The mercy rule does not apply, and one
can't simply toss the glove and walk away,
give up his turn at bat. It isn't done.

Behind the backstop there's a garden hose
the players use to soak their heads. They're down
five runs. Wherever optimism goes
it's gone. The on-deck hitter acts the clown—

he pulls a length of hose up through his crotch,
lets fly a mighty, arcing, godlike piss.
The count is full. The diehards stand to watch
our last faint hope swing from the heels and miss.

Penseés Pourries

Empire makes for better art.
Armies from across the border
—helpful in restoring order—
benefit the poet too.
Epic needs a Bonaparte;
elegy, a Waterloo.

•

One illusion, shatterproof,
beats a row too-many-sided.
Who would want a house divided
seeing that it cannot stand?
Best to sleep beneath one roof,
milk-fed in the motherland.

•

Those with nothing risk it all.
Dust to dust, haphazard, drifting
any way the wind is shifting,
Everyman's a floating speck
far too light to take a fall:
save your breath and save your neck.

•

Give to Caesar what is mine.
Once the statues are erected
people know what is expected,
everybody's better served.
Kafka only liked to whine.
Nervous men become unnerved.

•

Aphrodite, amputee.
Master*pieces,* cracks the cynic.
Hell, the Louvre should be a clinic:
Alexander's broken face,
Winged (but headless) *Victory*
carried here from Samothrace . . .

•

Priceless things can be restored;
replicas are manufactured
of the icon marred or fractured.
Ozymandias is dust?
Anybody can afford
Alexander's plastic bust.

•

Careless of what comes to pass,
poetry's a hothouse flower
blissfully removed from power,
self-abandoned, self-content,
blossoming behind the glass,
deaf to every argument.

•

Confident in knowing that
disciplined, impassive faces
see to things in higher places,
let us let our thoughts run wild.
Only the sad bureaucrat
reprimands his inner child.

•

Shout the loudest, fan the flames,
undermine the mediator,
urge the crowd to ever greater
ecstasies of self-contempt;
point the finger, naming names—
only hold yourself exempt.

Seeds

Summers at the zoo in Baltimore
the elephants are given watermelons.
Pleasure goes rippling through their tough hides.
You see it. Elephants are obvious.
They're made to traipse about savannas where
they trumpet their good spirits like rotund
and rosy husbands crooning in the shower.
The melons are so cool and green, they love them.
They wrap their trunks around them, raise them up
and smash them on the hard-packed earth.
You'd need an Africa to house such gladness then—
they bring the pieces to their mouths; they slurp them;
they eat up everything, the rinds and all.

There is a saying: *The eating of a melon
will produce a thousand good works.* So
these elephants have got it in them now
to build a Taj Mahal. They're keen to start
transporting heavy stones. All for love
they store up reservoirs of dawns. It's possible
to work for days, shining from within.
Illustrious projects stem from their delight.
The elephants grow big with what's alive
in their great hearts, that hard, bright seed—the sun!—
whose vigor draws the melon from the vine.

Animal Psalms

for Samuel Menashe

The Skunk
Psalm 23

I am anointed too,
brushed with his broad mark.
He leads me safely through
the alley in the dark.

The Sheep
Psalm 119

Tepid, woolly, I stray,
leaving the path behind me.
It's really the best way:
my shepherd's glad to find me.

The Bee
Psalm 19

I sense him everywhere,
like pollen far-flung,
heavy on the air
as sweetness on the tongue.

Reading French

Even if it all came back to me,
I'd have a six-year-old's vocabulary,
three hundred words of Québécois patois
specific to a town or maybe two
along the Merrimac. They wouldn't be
the same a little farther up the river,
were anyone around to speak them now.
I'm left with the impression of a language
underneath the one I've learned to use,
some useless wrinkles on the cerebrum,
impractical as love. An undertone
that surfaces in lullabies and hymns,
the books that adults read aloud to children,
the makeshift first few syllables of poems,
the feverish letter that gets thrown away
before the end of time makes good its promise—
any kind of speech that lets the sound
carry the greater part of what is said.

I read, though haltingly, a little French,
alert to what might be the echo of
that sound. *Le Nouveau Testament,* for instance.
I know the story well enough to guess
the meaning of the unfamiliar phrases.
My lack of fluency is helpful, though.

The ancient words attributed to Jesus
gather to themselves a fullness when
I cannot glance at them and understand.
If only for a moment, they retain
their substance, resting in the sounds they are,
holding the shapes they take as they are spoken.
They are like rounded stones beneath my feet;
a clear, cold water rushes over them.
And I can hear it. I remember when
I knelt beside my mother in the night,
all our prayers were made of words like these.

The Regular

Under her green apron the baby shifts
its weight as she puts on a smile to greet
the next in line. She jots the hieroglyphs
inside the boxes on the cup: 2 Sweet-
'N-Lo with 1% and not too hot.
No interest in something from the case.
She takes the card and slides it through the slot.
Thank you, and another pleasant face
for Mr. Hamilton, a regular
in sombre suit and tie, the funeral home
director. "Put this in your baby jar."
She marks his single latte, extra foam,
as he pays up, leaving the tip. A ten.
And he'll be back. He's not like other men.

Division of Labor

The first man dreams away his afternoons,
a second plays with words. A third's in charge
of central metaphor; a fourth communes
with Nature. Fifth, ambassador-at-large,
seeks images on far, exotic shores;
another sinks his heels into the soil.
A seventh does the punctuation chores;
an eighth supplies emotional turmoil.
The ninth man burns a candle to the muse,
the tenth keeps count to get the meter right.
Eleven finds an editor to schmooze
while twelve becomes acquainted with the night.
This man's peculiar business is in tropes.
Apprentices address the envelopes.

Against Beauty

Insubstantial, light, poetical,
like sea-tossed lace, the clouds float down the air.
And so with gray-green eyes, and wind-swept hair;
youth is a cosmetic for the skull.

Neither is beauty safe for being brief.
Better imprisoned in a narrow cell
than in the whorls of beauty's stippled shell
which, endlessly becoming, come to grief,

murmuring still of blue tides coming in.
Beauty draws the diver past the shelf,
a danger unto others and oneself.
Beauty is a burden on the skin.

Crouch

Lonesome wants to be left alone.
Needy doesn't know how to ask.
Stammer stares at the telephone.
Savage wears an impassive mask.

Lonesome stands in the empty lane.
Needy talks to himself aloud.
Stammer looks for the words in vain.
Savage enters the faceless crowd.

Lonesome sleeps but he doesn't dream.
Needy dreams but he doesn't sleep.
Stammer loses his self-esteem.
Savage readies to take the leap.

Levieux Gets the Best of His Better Sense

She warmed to me; I'll live another day.
I'll love another time, apparently.
You're older than her dad, who passed away.
Try not to bring that up again, okay?—
this hour begins a golden age, for me.
Or better, silver. Something close to gray.

She works in town. The sun and I gave chase.
Her heels rose up the elevator shaft.
You're out of breath, poor man, red in the face.
You've climbed two flights already. Quit the race.
She glanced my way in passing and she laughed.
Her sigh secured my heart in its embrace.

Not every exhalation is a sigh.
And every fool who's gladdest when he's fooled
is sadder when he's wiser by and by.
Then I'll resolve to grow no wiser. I
am not a schoolboy, granted. Why be schooled?
I've insufficient flesh to mortify.

The Adversary's Adages

There're better devils than the one you know.
We catch our flies with vinegar. We teach
old gods new tricks. We ruin before we walk.
Our ignorance is cheap; our bliss is talk.
The truth wears out. We fracture what we preach:
judge the tree where money doesn't grow.
Waste and want. Gut the golden goose.
Or spill the milk and cry, *No use! No use!*

One I have we; the blind have made us king.
Blood is thicker than skin deep, you see.
Where there's a wake, be keen to read the will.
Shoot the messenger. There's time to kill.
What's done cannot be said so easily.
Those born to hang are drowning: drink and sing.
The skull laughs best who grins from ear to ear.
Fear itself is all we have, my dear.

Mason Gardner Sold His Place

Mason Gardner sold the home
all his paths had started from;
unpropitious circumstance
forced him to remove at once.

So he tidied up the place,
settled on the fairest price,
boxed his clothes and paid the bills,
found an address somewhere else.

When the back and forth was done,
still he stayed to mow the lawn,
cart the fallen branches off,
nail new shingles to the roof

(as if money were no object),
organize his books by subject
as he put them on the curb,
needing time to let absorb

his displacement from the hearth
(time will tell what time is worth).
Cleaned the chimney, oiled the hinges,
set to work on making changes

oft-postponed for this or that
reasonable reason but
now at last prioritized—
planed the side door where it seized,

trimmed the wayward hedges back,
painted rails, repointed brick,
making certain all was well.
Projects more ambitious still

needed his attention then;
he was not an idle man.
Anxious that the closing date
not arrive before he got

things arranged as they should be,
he kept at it night and day,
sacrificing sleep to dream,
picturing what he might frame.

Walking with a measured step,
patiently he drew a map
outlining the garden beds,
fields beyond, and then the woods,

labeling the hills and trees,
places where the deer would graze,
where the owl liked to sit
and the eagle's habitat.

Here the raccoon washed its meal,
here were chestnuts in the fall,
here a crossing made of planks.
Careful here. Watch out for skunks.

Mostly pleasures, few alarms
(prickly patches, mayfly swarms)
dotted his topography;
ornate arrows showed the way

picnickers might take to find
berries blanketing the ground,
pointed out (for when it rained)
spots protected from the wind,

noted where the shade was best,
limbs a tired child could trust,
fiddleheads in early spring,
or the mossy overhang

giving on the green Great Marsh
"wild as Mary's secret wish!"
(Mason got that from a song
heard but once when he was young.)

Sketching in the poplar trees
Mason paused to rest his eyes,
walked out to the patio,
grateful for the longer view

from the Adirondack chair
towards the field's edge, where the deer,
silent in the quiet dusk,
passed like questions one might ask

in and swiftly out of mind
to the darker woods beyond.
"Here's exactly where to sit
when you are unsure of Fate."

(Mason in his chair is staring
past the woods, and past the clearing.
Eager buds that crowd the season
blur and tincture the horizon,

haze ascending from the bay
where the ocean meets the sky,
till mere sight decides on faith
water, air, or wash of both.)

Four AM, and still he sat,
May the first, the dreaded date,
cool, clear water in his hand,
waiting for the world to end.

"Mason Gardner, look around you.
Look before you, look behind you.
Stars give way. The seedlings stir.
Oh, there is no leaving here."

When the new owners arrived,
in the driveway freshly paved
stood another moving van:
Mason Gardner moving in!

Was there some misunderstanding?
Gardner's tenure should be ending.
Had he not been such a prince,
there'd have followed arguments,

disappointment and confusion.
Who would entertain the notion
that a man who'd sold his home
should yet occupy a room?

Graciously he made his case
so it sounded neat and nice,
more like help and company;
he would not be in the way:

he had plans to paint the shed,
plant a hedge along the road,
splice the tea rose ... One fine day
resurrect the apple tree ...

Worried She May Be the One

A quiet afternoon. I'll celebrate
this last occasion of my loneliness.
Spread before me, it should last awhile,
like snow in April, weathering her smile
and her bright heat, becoming ever less
my own, my unenchanting opiate,
my carpet magic won't make fly around,
my dirty blanket frozen to the ground.

But why should I regret to see erased
these bare twigs scratched in pencil on the air?
Why should I linger at the threshold musing
backward? What have I to lose in losing
nothing—gone missing from the nothing there?
Who'd want his part of emptiness replaced?

Planning a Rescue

First, find someone in need of one.
If you find yourself near water,
you know where to look. Your son,
maybe—maybe your lover's daughter—

will have drifted out too far.
Will the moonlit surface hold?
Hard to tell from where you are.
Hard to see what you are told

by way of gesture, silhouette,
shadows moving at a crawl.
You may get your collar wet
with no one swimming there at all.

•

Be watchful of high places, too,
office buildings, bridges, wells ...
Wells are not high places, true.
They're deep, and deep is something else.

Either toss a coin inside
and make a wish to have it back,
or wish to have that wish denied
and wish for something else you lack.

But if you wish to save the kind
for whom the lack of footing's thrilling,
you've got to seize him from behind;
he must be rescued all unwilling.

•

A ledge has something to attract
the man who feels misfortune calling;
he'll climb high as the odds are stacked
against him, where he'll dream of falling

because it feels like flying or
because it feels like letting go,
like something he's been waiting for,
a feeling that he used to know.

Though his prospects may be dim,
one step will get him clear of debt.
You're taking that away from him
when you come running with a net.

•

It's difficult to let the lost
meander any way they choose,
preferring that to being bossed;
hard to watch the loser lose

and hold your tongue, and let him think
he's getting somewhere up ahead.
But we'd as soon come to the brink
as we would let ourselves be led.

If the gods could trade their places
with us travelers here below,
they would seldom lift their faces
to ask the straightest way to go.

•

It can be unpleasant, saving
people who are desperate.
They're apt to think their misbehaving
is the very thing for it.

Let's save a man from being drowned.
Be careful if he's one of those
who tends to swing his arms around.
You'll catch an elbow to the nose.

Hook your arm around his chest.
It's almost like a wrestling match.
You have to hope you wrestle best.
The drowned are murder to detach.

Free Stuff

I'm tossing out ideas for poems
grown too familiar to inspire.
These sparks could still ignite a fire;
they only need to find new homes.
Food for thought that's going to waste
may satisfy another's taste.

Some titles that I've set aside:
    Crushing the Homunculus,
    Levitation on the Bus,
    Choirs of Angels Amplified,
    Riffing on Aquinas' Summa,
    Interview with Montezuma...

Personae destined for Goodwill:
    Antimidas the Alchemist,
    Kilroy the Ubiquitist,
    The *other* barber of Seville,
    William Wordsworth new-reborn
    and suckled in a creed outworn...

And topics worth one last hurrah:
    Samuel Johnson's question whether
    one dream may stand in for another;
    Picasso and dyslexia;
    Melville's embarrassment to be
    a grown man writing poetry...

Believe You Me

*I cannot wrap my brain around
how different you are from me.*
What difference? You make it sound
like crossing the Sargasso Sea
would take less effort than to find
where both of us are of one mind.

*If there were only two of us
the crosswind wouldn't be as strong.
There's you and me to ferry, plus
the third you always bring along.
That's our Bermuda triangle.
We sink because the boat's too full.*

*My own decisions are my own.
I don't let others think for me.
I don't rely on the Unknown.
I take responsibility.
Before you act, you run it by
the great Commander in the sky.*

For my part, I don't understand
why you should care what I believe.
One can't "think freely" on demand.
Not every kind of faith's naive.
Whoever wants to see what is
has got to look past surfaces.

And let me guess how that is done.
Shutting your eyes to what is there,
you see—though you're the only one—
a world you conjure from thin air.
You don't perceive Reality.
You just see what you want to see.

Photographers will sometimes squint
to better read a value range.
I focus too, to catch a glint
of diamond-light that doesn't change
when most of what we're taking in
winds up in the recycling bin.

Oh, please! The things you're telling me
are even worse than I supposed.
I think this "diamond-light" you see
when you have got your eyes half-closed
gets in through where your brain is cracked,
and that explains the way you act.

You're making fun of what I said.
How do I act? Inform me, please.
Like you've got tinfoil on your head
tuned in to alien frequencies.
All right, it sounds absurd to say . . .
But you believe it anyway.

Bad Head Day

> *We shall never heap enough insults*
> *on the unruliness of our mind.*
> —Michel de Montaigne

More like a homing pigeon than an eagle,
off on anyone's errand, flying low;
mere hummingbird, one sip and there you go
to taste another colored bit of treacle;
hoarder of tickets, clippings and receipts;
peddler of small favors, trinketeer;
loser at Chutes and Ladders played for keeps,
darting on an impulse or in fear;
flip-flopper, window-shopper, Old Unreliable;
pliable, driveling swivel-neck; train wreck;
besotted pothead at the salad bar
mistaking the couscous for caviar;
poetaster spitting up inanities,
or making perfect mermaids out of manatees;
an awful lot of nothing in the aggregate;
paralegal for the devil's advocate.

Genius Is Only Good for What It's Good For

Stocks in the South Sea Company climbed to 1,000 British pounds before falling to nothing in 1720. A massive amount of money was lost.

The stiff who breaks his back to make ends meet
believes if he were smarter he'd be rich.
He'd climb out of his rut and find his niche.
More brains would put him in the driver's seat;
soon he'd be getting places on The Street—
going for broke would go without a hitch.
He'd toss the T-shirt printed "Life's a Bitch."
He'd wear the one declaring "Life is Sweet!"

Sir Isaac Newton, though, found out too late
that he was bright enough "to calculate
the motions of celestial spheres, but not
the madness of the people." He too bought
shares in the soaring South Sea Company,
ignoring what he knew of gravity.

Applicant Evaluation: Thomas, Dylan

Position applied for: Space left blank.
Skills specific to the job: n/a.
Reference: You'll have yourself to thank.
Related education: Hard to say.
Appearance: Unkempt; thick around the jowls.
Communication skills: Opaque but fluid;
authoritative larynx, good with vowels.
Previous employment: Sometime Druid,
with background in syllabic inventory,
trained at rinsing wisdom off the pearls.
Strengths: Banter, bonhomie. Can tell a story.
Weaknesses: Brown ale and ready girls.
Health: Golden. In his heyday, knock on wood.
Regular habits: Yes, but not all good.

Persnickety Ichabod, Class of '74

I went to the reunion. Don't ask why.
I got the invitation, told them I
would just as soon we kept a little distance,
but soon grew tired of hearing their insistence,

deleting all the e-mail that they sent,
so I broke down, and got dressed up, and went
to eat some chicken in a function room
and find out what their séance might exhume.

The years made dull-boy Jack a full-grown bore
and he was there to greet me at the door.
He talked about a girl I used to date
whom he'd been chatting up. "She's looking great."

He did something peculiar with his lips
and something early Elvis with his hips.
At once I was transported to the present.
"Yes. Right. Well, she must have found *that* pleasant."

I rummaged in my Social Crisis Kit
for something more than *Difficulty Hearing;*
excused myself to stage a *Coughing Fit*
when I had no success with *Disappearing;*

looked over people's heads to find the bar.
They flag you down. They ask you how you are.
You're everybody's buddy, chum, amigo . . .
It's a back-slapping gauntlet for the ego.

You smile like mad. You hustle, ill at ease,
to beat the market trading pleasantries
while running toward what you're running from:
the man you would avoid you have become.

An Innocence

Like Robert Burns, I too turn up a nest
while working, raking last year's leaves in spring.
But not a mouse. Pale rabbits, shivering,
rustled from their blind and naked rest.
If they showed fright, I'd feel it in my chest,
but only shying from the chill, they cling
together close, alive as anything,
three steps from Route 1A. Unwelcome guest,
I have surprised them in their nursery,
stumbling on the bed and canopy
their diligent though absent mother built,
with muzzle-fashioned, straw-and-lapin quilt,
but I am less disturbance than a flea.
They focus on the task at hand. To be.

Doctor B___

Most alert when I least need to be
(My young wife tosses in her sleep and sighs),
I sit upright in bed, awake at three,
as real events elude my mental grip
and turn to dreams. The line between them blurs.
And if my waking hours are transient stuff—
if days are lost to memory soon enough—
this hour is when the uprising occurs.
The dreams that I would willingly let slip
take hold. I don't know where they're bringing me.
Familiar things put on a thin disguise
in passages too dimly lit to see.

And here is where I end up. Where I am.
Without a sense of how I've gotten here.
A dollar on the sidewalk. A stray lamb.
I can't forget my dream about forgetting.
My family doctor's name had slipped my mind.
Awake and out of bed to get a drink,
I couldn't fix the loss, I couldn't think
of the guy's name. I started to rewind
the tape, to put his face within its setting,
I went in for a physical exam—
leaving my body—with a guilty fear
painfully tightening my diaphragm.

I'd gone to him for years. He was a friend.
What if I should meet him on the street?
How would I say hello? Would I pretend
to be distracted? (Would it be pretense?)
Next morning, after coffee, still a blank.
But I refused to check my address book
and give in, I forbade myself to look
through all the B's. (That far I'd gotten, thank
God, yes—a B. The fog was not as dense
around that letter.) I resolved to spend
the whole day rather than accept defeat,
declare my last brain-wrinkle a dead end

before I'd look for help from anyone.
That too, though, gave me pause. Here I'm afraid
that early-onset Alzheimer's begun,
that I'll be old too soon—I start to act
like any elderly and failing man,
stubborn and fiercely fearful of assistance,
who only wants the nurse to keep her distance.
He moves the furniture to prove he can,
by throwing all his strength against the fact
of his decline. The bureau weighs a ton.
He's still defending a mistake he made
this afternoon while talking to his son.

Someday I won't remember my own name—
Everyman is no one in a while.
Throw my important papers on the flame:
a flare of heat, a blackening, a flight
of something falling into nothing more.
These ashes are a stage along the way.
I have forgotten what I meant to say.
I have forgotten what I came here for.
I have forgotten to turn off the light.
I have forgotten how to play the game.
I have forgotten how to make her smile.
I wanted everything to stay the same.

Ellipse

restless, off center, again, so often now it seems
a kind of starting point, familiar in its way,
a place I might come back to, on my own, could be
I shouldn't try to shake this, haven't lost my focus,
only that another has developed and
there's no one center now, I'm someone else as well,
this one and that one both, no need to come around

Cellar Snake

Since spring, I guess, we've shared the same address.
The snake's been living with us, more or less.
But we don't share a group mentality.
And we don't want him living here for free.

My slinking cat is equal to the task.
His eyes glow green behind a cobweb mask.
He can't be recognized when he appears
to occupants whose rent is in arrears.

The snake has got his tail between his legs.
In fact, he's got his legs between his tail—
he's got no knees to kneel on when he begs.
If the serpent's got a prayer, it's doomed to fail.

Already he's been turned back empty-handed.
Bent at an angle, cornered where he landed,
his shapely S is wrenched into an L.
But is the letter dead? It's hard to tell.

He seems to have a fatal bloody nose.
Beside him—clearer than you would suppose—
a little pool of liquid on the floor.
Too late, I think, to show him to the door.

I stand there doing nothing, like a god.
The cat can't wake his plaything with a prod
so he gets up and walks away. He's bored.
It's overrated, being overlord.

The Passional

The saints have got a sickly look.
As pale as death. Or paler.
He saw their pictures in a book
his aunt kept in her trailer.

He looked at St. Sebastian, caught
and tied up to a tree
with arrows in his neck. He thought,
"There's the life for me."

He wanted to have wounds like that
and suffer for the Lord.
He tried to irritate the cat.
It hurt to be ignored.

Sometimes he stood outdoors at night
without mosquito spray.
It made him think he'd rather fight
a lion any day.

Some martyrs get their bellies torn
to pieces in arenas.
He broke a brambleberry thorn.
He held it near his penis.

It's not as easy as it seems
to get a chance to die
and prove you're not the kind that screams
and almost starts to cry.

He wouldn't make a lot of fuss.
He'd face the evil forces
unruffled as Hippolytus
yanked apart by horses.

Mid-November House Guest

Because he never seems to move, I wonder
how he got to where he's standing still.
The slow, painstaking insect barely flinches
when I touch his eyelash-like antenna.
He started toward stopping hours ago:
his life's a drawn-out pilgrimage of inches.
No fretful vacillation of the will,
no panic, no unthinking flight, no blunder
out of the frying pan into Gehenna.
He's acting on an instinct to be slow.

This afternoon he idles on *The Globe,*
mingling with the newsprint. The headlines treat him
like the frivolous calligraphy
he seems. Two columns forge the long decline
he's clawed to, elbowing his spindly serif,
as if they mean to spell calamity.
One day soon, his end will come to meet him.
No exoskeletal thanatophobe,
he stands his ground and calmly holds the line,
as though supporting "Sullivan for Sheriff."

But I presume to know my guest too well:
anthropomorphism is impolite.
He's not The Fly, or Gregor Samsa's cousin.
He's not himself (though who am I to say?).
He doesn't want to do annoying things
I would expect of him, like swarmin', buzzin',
(dropping g's!). He stays inside at night,
retreating ever deeper in his shell.
He's shot. He's too far gone to fly away.
He's got the winter weighing on his wings.

January

Winds lay bare the nest
with its small, unbroken egg
of snow, sleeping in.

October 1962

"Up in the bathtub early..." Not at night.
"Get dressed, put on your brand new underwear..."
"Between your sisters on the couch, sit tight..."

"Come here a minute, let me comb your hair..."
This was an actual emergency,
although my baby brother didn't care

on mother's lap, where I wished I could be,
not looking at the television set.
Russia was gearing up for World War III

with JFK. Nobody'd shot him yet.
She spent the afternoon preparing us.
I guess we were prepared as we could get.

Maybe she pictured Mount Vesuvius?
Not an atom bomb, but still. The closest thing.
It would explain her making all the fuss.

She wouldn't quit, or waste time wondering
exactly what to do with one last day;
she planned for what the future still might bring

and tried to get us ready, in her way,
for when someone unburied our Pompeii.

Black Spinet

On a red and orange day
with many people in it
the new piano arrived—
a bird flew in the open
door—and a fat man's butt showed
above his belt as he leaned
to try to lift it himself,
before a gang of my uncles
tied some old jokes together
with brown twine and brown whiskey,
and somehow hoisted the thing
onto their wiry shoulders,
like a teetering coffin,
and came in through the hallway
where the crazed grackle fluttered
till, crashing the wallpaper,
it fell, stunned, and got stepped on.
My aunts called mother silly
for wanting a piano
or for some other reason
that got lost halfway upstairs,
where I watched through the railing.
Wind and leaves skittered outside.
The fat man got his money
knocking knickknacks to the floor,

drove his truck to Canada,
and they sent another man
in bow tie and suspenders,
a winker the ladies liked.
This one tuned the piano,
abracadabra, like that,
with a flourish of nimble
fingers even the uncles
admired while poking fun,
and stayed through supper without
eating any meat pie or
ever swallowing the green
drink balanced on two black keys
his light hands hopped on their way
up and down the run of scales,
like two sparrows quarreling
back and forth on a long limb.
The aunts heard their requests through
explosions of gaiety,
rocking the couches, singing
with impossible voices.
Their funny lipstick faded
while the curtained night air
whispered softest hints of red
and the darkness grew warmer.
An elderly gentleman
without a cane or body

gracefully led my mother
by the hand through the night to
a spot near mine on the porch,
on the swinging couch so old
it had grown invisible.
Another music played there.

Eel

The year the dam collapsed the lake slid back.
Its wide, slow stream moved through a realm of mud
that dried and cracked, a maze of intersecting
faults I studied, peering under stones.

Spiders the size of golf balls ran away,
white ones and black ones. Wraiths of vapor rose;
the earth was groaning in a fevered sleep.

I brought a safety pin and ball of string.
Driving a stake into the clay, I cast
the makeshift hook into a pool, let out
the string, and left it overnight—no bait—
expecting that its glint would draw the flash
of something weighty burrowed in the silt.

I worried centipedes and larvae from
their purgatories with a stick, and gladly
plashed in scum to find the leopard frog.

Meanwhile, the miracle was incubating.
Reeling in the kitchen twine at last
I felt a living shudder running through!

As quickly as I spooled the string around
an open hand, my expectation mounted,
and maybe once I felt again a tug,
a quickening, though uncertain, maybe just
the dull resistance of a clump of weeds;
a snag it may have been, that I'd imagined
having teeth and eyes. A tangled line
another fisherman had lost was caught
and dragging on my futile safety pin,
but when I'd hauled its looping ravels in
I saw that yet another fishing line
was knotted to the first—this could go on—
a hidden random mesh connecting me
with something suddenly, ferociously
alive and thrumming through its many threads!

The snaky glaucous monster of a fish
broke through the surface thrashing and submerged
again, recoiling in the bottom murk.
The water took the shape of him and stirred.
I had him on a leash! I stuffed the snarl
beneath a rock and ran to get a pail.
My lungs on fire in my chest, I knelt
to hoist the eel out of its element.

•

When I went out to check, ten times a day,
it hadn't died. It circled in the pail.
Or else it died and circled anyway.
The teeth were right up close behind the tail.

The Convert

When Brandon first began to think, he thought
he'd wait for an idea to come to mind.
Idea-like, phrases sauntered in. A lot—
but ragged, motley, not the brilliant kind.

The spark of light he'd been anticipating
never showed. He sat there in a fog.
Till finally Brandon grew impatient, waiting,
weary of his inner monologue.

So when The Master said the things he said,
and tore the idols down, and all the rest,
a naked bulb went on inside his head.
The first idea he'd ever heard expressed

with passion marked him with its fiery brand,
so he began to think the one same thought
unchanging, one that few could understand.
And whether that is thinking or it's not,

he wasn't isolated anymore.
He could participate in mythopoeia.
He liked the uniforms the soldiers wore
who marched in service of the one idea.

The one idea. It occupied his mind
the way an army occupies a city.
Set him on edge. Gave him an ax to grind
that cut through fleshly sentiment and pity.

Gave him a plan, with nothing left to chance.
A blazing lamp, exposing the denier.
A lens to focus on the stream of ants
the heathen are. Until they all catch fire.

Triptych

1.

Here is a portrait by F. Appleton,
whose name is unfamiliar. The subject is
Royal Artillery Lieutenant-Colonel
Henry Shrapnel. Painted in 1812,
the officer's thin lips and steady gaze
project the moral strength and self-assurance
requisite for one in his position.
His actual position, though, is vague.
His elbow rests on an amorphous bulge
protruding from the background of the painting,
or else it rests uncomfortably on nothing.
The forearm would appear too short, the hand
detached and dangling lifeless from the cuff.
On second glance, the oval head itself
looks set in place, the collar like an egg cup.
The pitch-black stiffness of the uniform
conceals too well the man who's wearing it,
whose parts don't seem to form a whole. Most likely
the uniform was painted first—brass buttons,
those striking British-Army-red lapels—
and only afterward the face and hand.
The officer would not have had to sit
neglecting his responsibilities

too long. Someone else could take his place.
In any case, what was of interest to
the painter must have been the uniform.
The braided epaulet on the right shoulder,
finger-like, seems poised to crawl away.
Brass buttons, golden ornament, the shirt
a burst of white carnation at the throat.
And all that red exploding on the eye.

2.

An image of Mikhail Kalashnikov
posing with the AK-47.
His jaw is firm, his hair is combed straight back,
his eyes are those the ancient sculptors cast
in bronze, expressive in their emptiness.
He wears a pleated military jacket.
The butt end of the rifle snug against
an epaulet with one gold star, the barrel
tilts toward the upper right-hand corner
of the photograph. Positioned underneath
the front sight-post, on top of the piano,
a camel figurine tugs at its harness.
Another object on the polished surface,
made of tinted glass, may represent
a female figure, elegant and tall.
A chair is pulled back from the instrument,

as though someone sat down to play, then closed
the cover down over the keys. The grain
of the veneer stands out. Against the wall,
potted flowers peek from behind the weapon,
pink and frail beside the signature
curve of the magazine, presented to
view with a craftsman's pride, the focus of
this portrait, taken in the living room
of what appears to be a modest home.

3.

We'll hear Beethoven's opus 27,
no. 2, performed by Edward Teller.
This is a video recording made
at Stanford in September 1990,
in the professor's home on campus. Not
a moment's wasted. Teller strikes the keys
the very instant we click PLAY, and keeps
the tempo up to reach the final chord
three minutes and four seconds afterward.
No mooning. Rubinstein took twice as long.
Despite the hurried pace, the pianist
appears to ruminate; he works his jaw
in time with the arpeggios. No one
is in the room with him, except perhaps
the cameraman, who stays out of the picture.

Irregular white strips of sunlight mark
the painted walls and darker paneling.
There are green plants in baskets near the window.
Teller wears a ring on his right hand.
Nearing two minutes into the recording,
he turns the page of music. We zoom in on
his face, beaded now with perspiration.
Drops roll slowly down his nose and cheek.
His dark-rimmed glasses press against his temple.
His hair is mussed a little on this side.
The focus moves away again, the piece
winds to a close. A glance our way, a word;
he folds the music shut. The screen goes black.

How to Ignore an Invisible Man

Turn away briskly when sensing him near.
Brush off the whisper that tickles your ear.
Keep to the middle of sidewalks and hallways
or he'll sidle up next to you, once and for always.

Quietly tidy the rooms he leaves cluttered
and wipe up the crumbs of the toast that he buttered.
Remove empty hangers you find in the closet.
Give him the slip when you make a deposit.

Don't worry if someone keeps tracking in mud;
remember that water is thinner than blood.
Keep up appearances, try to relax;
appearance is something your nemesis lacks.

The trouble, of course, with these men without faces,
is that they are standing in line to trade places.
They make you uncomfortable, cramped in your skin.
If you choose to step out, they are quick to slip in.

- You notice your signature isn't your own.
- You're told you don't sound like yourself on the phone.
- A friend calls you *Sir* while presenting his card.
- Your labrador chases you out of his yard.

The video stream of your ego is paused—
amazing how little disturbance is caused,
how no one reports this identity theft.
Who'd claim to be victimized? No one is left.

The Guitar Maker

for Herbert Clancey

Like the signature in maple wood
      of sun-splashed rain,
this man's bright *pattern* must remain
beside the workbench where he stood
      smoothing the grain.

Deprived of work, he would not rest
      for fidgeting;
he lived to build a living thing
that, by impassioned hands caressed,
      might learn to sing.

This shop is where his spirit is.
      Twelve months a year,
the world arranged to meet him here,
arriving in trussed packages
      from far and near.

Rosewood came from India,
      mahogany
from the Caribbean sea,
and from western Africa
      came ebony.

Tonewoods from earth's four corners sent
    he stacked here, stored
beneath an image of Our Lord,
    who made of him the instrument
        of their accord.

One Day

We walked in light and shade
along the lichened wall,
no task at hand
and nothing planned.
The poplar branches swayed.
And Finlay chased his ball.

And something made us smile,
and something else, again.
Nothing less
than happiness,
and good to last awhile.
Enough to last till when . . .

This simple summer day
of not too much to do
may be the one
we look back on
when years have swirled away
and days like these are few.

Sacred Spring

for Gina

  We don't expect too much
  from visiting the rocks
at Glanum: broken pillars, crumbling walls and such,
  a pile of tumbled blocks

  without a leaf of shade,
  unburied in the sun
to bleach again; a scene too colorless to fade,
  a past that's gone and done.

  But following the guide
  we stop to see what's next:
a place oddly familiar, as though we've stepped inside
  a high school history text.

  We're not *un*welcome here,
  the sun is overhead;
the earth is dry, the air is still, the sky is clear;
  the neighborhood is dead.

    We wander aimlessly
        through porticoes and lanes.
It's like exploring someone else's memory,
        respectful, taking pains

        to leave things as they are.
        I find you on a stair,
leaning to look down into the reservoir.
        A shaded pool is there.

        You're thoroughly immersed.
        Little fish, I think,
or else what has you rooted there is ancient thirst—
        your soul has stopped to drink.

        These are the healing waters,
        it says in the brochure.
And does the mother-goddess whisper to her daughters?
        Again, I can't be sure.

Genius

So I go out to get the mail
at one o'clock, always one o'clock
because it's such a disappointment
getting there before the postman does
to find the mailbox empty, coupled with
the everyday discouragement of
not receiving word from the MacArthur
people telling me I'm one of
this year's geniuses-in-waiting,
and what is there for me today?
A postcard made to look like an antique,
an illustration of a red guitar
against an off-white background with
the words You Rock My World
in black beneath the instrument.
On the other side, the message reads,
"I can't imagine how dull my life
would be without you, I love you!"
I feel afraid at first, the postcard
isn't signed, is this some complication
wrestling to the ground my happy
simple notion of my life? Will Gina
be upset? Only then I realize that
Gina sent the card herself! And
still I don't believe it. Her life would

not be dull without me. She'd flash
that smile in passing; some man
would buy a derby hat to wear
next time he ordered coffee
at her shop, invite her down to
stroll along the wharves and out
along a rope-plank bridge to
board his yacht just in from
oriental gardens—not the Chinese
restaurant, an Asian arboretum
planted near a Taoist temple
nearly halfway round the globe
where it is nighttime when it's
daytime here and everything's the
opposite of what you might expect
so there's no boredom possible
unlike with me, with my umbrella-
like forbearance and my ex-
planations of where "coolness"
had its origin: in heroin addiction,
because those jazzmen like Chet
Baker felt so chilly all the time
and had to wear a sweater in
the summer even, that and
the indifferent attitude of
someone like a William Burroughs
managing to look quite serious

and not ridiculous believing
stuff that we make fun of Tom
Cruise for believing. How is any of
that interesting to someone
fine like Gina? I love her
making that mistake, if even for
the moment that it took to
write the postcard, which she
didn't sign, by the way, she
maybe had misgivings at the
last minute, even so, she put it
in the mail, and I felt like
an honorary genius when
I finally got it figured out, as
though I'd been selected by
the grant committee, except for
of course the money part, but
hey, it's still enough to live on.

A Bother

Here's Rocco now, sprawling across the keys;
whatever I may try to write,
he's there in black and white,
purring, rolling on his back to bite
my fingers if he disagrees,
minding my q's and p's.

Well, I require constant stroking too.
And maybe I get in the way.
I like for you to say
I'm clever, good. And feed me twice a day.
There's nothing I would rather do
than rub up next to you

and feel that spark of electricity
leap at the touch, connecting you to me.

Why Bees Hum

The ancients say that Zeus so loved the bees
he made them golden like the sun,
imparting to each one
a ray of sacred fire, finely spun—
bright scarves in which they wouldn't freeze
when winter bared the trees.

Freed from the mortal fear of winter time,
whose threat the god had stooped to lift,
and grateful for the gift,
the bees spread out through autumn fields to drift
among the flowers, or cling and climb
and sip of the sublime

unhurried and unworried. Given heat,
they celebrate by making something sweet.

Nuts

I come in contact with a lot of nuts.
Poetry readings. Church. The library.
They're always there. Lost souls end up in ruts
like everybody else. I often see

a man whose armload of biographies
that codger won't live long enough to read,
fumbling for change to pay his past-due fees
on other *Lives*. How many does he need?

He's lost his place in his own story, one
thin volume more than he can carry home,
library-quiet, fording the Acheron.
And then there are the ruts that lead to Rome:

the crazies go to Mass on Sunday, too.
I've noticed torture going on. One fellow
brings the Inquisition to his pew.
His hair is matted, black. His eyes are yellow.

No "sign of peace." He won't let you come near.
His forehead's beaded from the fires he's fanning.
Blood storms. Paroxysms of guilt. I fear
his awful sin may be the one he's planning.

And poetry. Perhaps I shouldn't say.
The open mic's a magnet for the daft.
The trembling hand. The mangled, stiff cliché.
Time is a river; the podium's a raft

that poets grip, riding the floodwaters—let
the four winds blow! The struggling poets row
against the swells, bedraggled, cold and wet.
Forgive them, for they know not where they go.

Alfred Nicol's book of poetry, *Elegy for Everyone,* published in 2009, was chosen for the first Anita Dorn Memorial Prize as "a work of complex vision and stylistic mastery." He received the 2004 Richard Wilbur Award for an earlier volume, *Winter Light,* of which Jay Parini wrote, "This is certainly among the finest new volumes of poetry I have read in years."

Nicol has written lyrics in French and English for nine original compositions by classical/flamenco guitarist John Tavano. Their CD, *The Subtle Thread,* released in January, 2015, has received airplay on WMBR's program *French Toast.*

Nicol's poems have appeared in *Poetry, The Hopkins Review, Dark Horse, First Things, The New England Review, Commonweal, The Formalist,* and other literary journals, as well as in *Contemporary Poetry of New England* and other anthologies.

Animal Psalms was a finalist for the 2015 Able Muse Book Award.

Also from Able Muse Press

William Baer, *Times Square and Other Stories*

Melissa Balmain, *Walking in on People – Poems*

Ben Berman, *Strange Borderlands – Poems*

Ben Berman, *Figuring in the Figure – Poems*

Michael Cantor, *Life in the Second Circle – Poems*

Catherine Chandler, *Lines of Flight – Poems*

William Conelly, *Uncontested Grounds – Poems*

Maryann Corbett,
Credo for the Checkout Line in Winter – Poems

John Philip Drury, *Sea Level Rising – Poems*

D.R. Goodman, *Greed: A Confession – Poems*

Margaret Ann Griffiths,
Grasshopper – The Poetry of M A Griffiths

Katie Hartsock, *Bed of Impatiens – Poems*

Elise Hempel, *Second Rain – Poems*

Jan D. Hodge, *Taking Shape – carmina figurata*

Ellen Kaufman, *House Music – Poems*

Emily Leithauser, *The Borrowed World – Poems*

Carol Light, *Heaven from Steam – Poems*

April Lindner, *This Bed Our Bodies Shaped – Poems*

Martin McGovern, *Bad Fame – Poems*

Jeredith Merrin, *Cup – Poems*

Richard Newman,
All the Wasted Beauty of the World – Poems

Frank Osen, *Virtue, Big as Sin – Poems*

Alexander Pepple (Editor), *Able Muse Anthology*

Alexander Pepple (Editor),
Able Muse – a review of poetry, prose & art
(semiannual issues, Winter 2010 onward)

James Pollock, *Sailing to Babylon – Poems*

Aaron Poochigian, *The Cosmic Purr – Poems*

John Ridland,
Sir Gawain and the Green Knight – Translation

Stephen Scaer, *Pumpkin Chucking – Poems*

Hollis Seamon, *Corporeality – Stories*

Carrie Shipers, *Embarking on Catastrophe – Poems*

Matthew Buckley Smith,
Dirge for an Imaginary World – Poems

Barbara Ellen Sorensen,
Compositions of the Dead Playing Flutes – Poems

Wendy Videlock, *Slingshots and Love Plums – Poems*

Wendy Videlock, *The Dark Gnu and Other Poems*

Wendy Videlock, *Nevertheless – Poems*

Richard Wakefield, *A Vertical Mile – Poems*

Gail White, *Asperity Street – Poems*

Chelsea Woodard, *Vellum – Poems*

www.ablemusepress.com

www.ingramcontent.com/pod-product-compliance
Lightning Source LLC
Chambersburg PA
CBHW031607110426
42742CB00037B/1321